Growing Through Grief

BreAnna Exum

BookLeaf Publishing

India | USA | UK

Presentation by *BookLeaf Publishing*

Web: www.bookleafpub.com

E-mail: info@bookleafpub.com

ISBN: 9789360941420

First edition 2024

This book is dedicated to my Daddy, Michael "Mike" Shumake, whom we tragically lost far too soon. He was a big factor within the book, as most of the poems have been inspired by his life, death, and painful absence.

Daddy, I pray you knew the impact you made on our lives and how much you will always mean to us. You'll never know how much we love and miss you.

May you rest in eternal peace.

ACKNOWLEDGEMENT

To my Momma - for always loving me, encouraging me, teaching me, fussing at me, and for telling me what I should do (even when you think I'm not listening).

To my little sister, Lyndria - who's always been my biggest answered prayer, inspiration, and someone I've always looked up to, both figuratively and literally (because it only makes sense that the younger sister is the tallest).

To my husband, Jason - for being my soulmate and best friend, for being my greatest supporter and biggest fan, for always believing in me, for never giving up on me, and for loving me the most when I can't figure out how to love myself.

I love you all so very much.

My Love

I remember the days I prayed for this -
the love I found in you.
I was so desperate to find what I have now,
I thought every guy was "the one".
I didn't have a clue.

I then begged for the attention I now receive
freely.
I tried to force it, even when I knew it wouldn't
work.
Over and over, I allowed myself to lose tears and
sleep.
They were the textbook definition of 'jerk'.

We rarely argue, and if we do, grudges are not
held for long.
You apologize freely and without hesitation.

You're the first to admit if you were out of line
or in the wrong.

You love me completely, and on my worst days,
you somehow love me even more.
You're my sun in the sky.
You're my moon so bright.
You make me keep going, even when I don't
want to try.

My one and only.
My matching soul and heart.
You're my greatest supporter.
I pray we never part.

Without you by my side, I refuse to exist.
I can't imagine having to live my life alone.
Where you go, I will always follow.
Wherever you are, I know I'm home.

Dear Food

All my life I've been a binge eater,
a fad diet believer,
and a diet pill junkie.
I've turned every which way in life,
except away from the table.
I've never been able.
It's been my constant in good times and bad.
It's the longest relationship I've ever had.
It's been my biggest enemy.
It helps me cope and helps me mend.
It's been here from the very start;
it'll probably kill me in the end.
Dear Food, I hate you.
You're my best friend.

Something in my brain never clicked quite right,
I think about it all the time;

every day and every night.
Fear of missing the experience,
fear of missing out on the taste,
making sure to clean my plate,
food's so expensive to let it go to waste.
It's been my biggest enemy.
It helps me cope and helps me mend.
It's been here from the very start;
it'll probably kill me in the end.
Dear Food, I hate you.
You're my best friend.

I'm not sure when it became an addiction,
I need that sugar-high infliction.
It may not be cocaine, but the sugar in my veins
is just as deadly.
I know I have the tendency to make excuses
about my dependency.
One day it'll catch up with me in the end.
Dear Food, I hate you.
You're my best friend.

"Chocolate helps me mend every heartbreak."
"It's fine because it's your birthday."
"If you don't eat, they'll think you're being rude."
"Eat this. It'll help that nasty attitude."
"Calories never count on the holidays."
Guilt-tripping your stomach with what others
say...

Counting calories, counting carbs,
meal replacement shakes and protein bars,
weight loss groups and OEAs,
weighing myself every single day,
learning to eat without feeling ashamed.
Maybe one day I won't worry about what others
have to say.
It's been my biggest enemy.
It helps me cope and helps me mend.
It's been here from the very start;
it'll probably kill me in the end.
Dear Food, I hate you.
You're my best friend.

Two Pink Lines

This is for my girls,
all my girls who know.
All my girls, we're floating in the
SAME DAMN BOAT.
We've been here a while, and the water is
CLEAR AS MUD.
What's worked for them just hasn't worked for
us...

They've got diapers, bottles, up-all-nighters,
stuffed toys, pacifiers,
first words, first steps, and nap time,
sing-alongs, and nursery rhymes...
We're still waiting on two pink lines.

I hear what you say.
I know how you feel.
You get online and someone else is pregnant,
WHAT'S THE DEAL?!?
They say it's in the water.
They say it's in the air.
It must be true, you see big ol' bellies
EVERYWHERE!
This wasn't in the plan;
not how it was supposed to go.
I'm here to tell you, in this battle you're not
alone.

They've got PTA, football games, homework,
and school plays,
4-H, Girl Scouts, and band practice times,
home late, and to bed by nine...
We're still waiting on two pink lines.

The unsolicited advice, that's what hurts.
"You should change your diet."
"Exercise more."
"Go to church."
The personal questions, they never end.
"You're not getting any younger, when are you
going to finally have some kids?"
"Is it you or him?"
"Have you tried this..."

Yeah, we know, just relax and don't think about
it...
You have to bite your tongue when you want to
scream.
It seems funny to me that everyone you know
has a PhD.

They have driver's license, prom, and
graduation,
first job, and college orientation.
Sure seems funny how time flies...
We're still waiting on two pink lines.

I'm Only Human

I've always had more awkwardness than beauty.
I often use humor to mask my pain.
My anxiety usually gets the best of me.
The little white pill helps to keep my depression
at bay.

I've never been the sweet center of attention.
Now that I'm older, I'd rather it stay that way.
I can't look you in the eyes.
Though, it's not because I'm shy,
it's fear of judgment with each word I say.

I've learned to just pick and choose my battles.
Simply put, confrontation isn't a friend of mine.
I've been accused of being aggressive in passing,
I don't realize I'm doing it most of the time.

I can point out my flaws rather quickly,
but constructive criticism is a hard tablet for me
to take.
It's amusing that my superiors say I'm eager to
develop.
Truthfully, I'm a people pleaser terrified of
making mistakes.

Errors are just a part of the process,
but I hate admitting that I'm weak.
I'd rather struggle in silence,
it's easier than accepting that it's help I need.

In the end, I'm only human;
composed of flesh and bone.
I'd rather face each day with foolishness,
than to know what the future holds.

Brooke

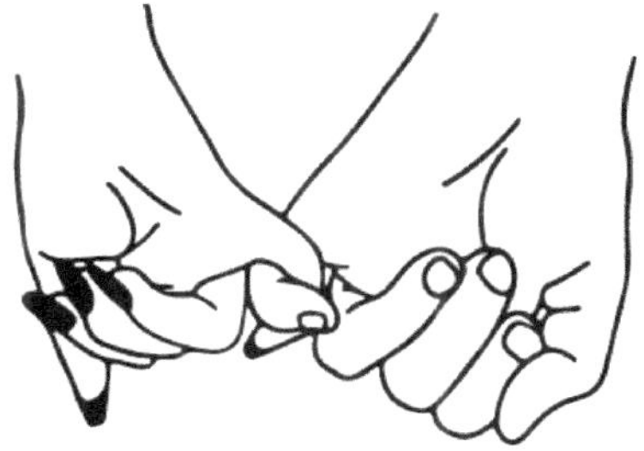

It hit me like a ton of bricks the moment I realized,
you walked away, but it wasn't quick,
yet, it happened right before my eyes.
I never saw you slipping away.
You never gave me any sign.
I didn't have a chance to beg you to stay.
You probably wouldn't have anyway.

We came from two different worlds but stood on common ground.
Our age gap was absurd, but in you, my person I found.
You kept me stable and level-headed.
I kept you young and wild.
We were side by side when home and about,
I never imagined this would be how our lives turned out.

Now, we're watching each other's life through a
phone screen.
I miss you.
Do you miss me?

16 and 26 - seems kind of odd.
We connected quickly, I thought we'd go far.
Side by side in different stages of life,
best friends by day,
P.I. stalking by night.
Standing solid through heartbreak and tears,
we know each other's deepest, darkest fears.
I love watching you succeed.
I'm just sad that it seems you don't need me
anymore.

I long for the times we spent together.
I miss the days of me and you -
Best Friends Forever.
If you only knew how I long for a warm
embrace,
or what I'd give to still be able to put a smile on
your face.
I wish I could find out where we fell apart.
I only want a conversation with a familiar heart.

I pray our story isn't over.
We had so many hopes and dreams when we
were younger.

Please say we don't end this way.
Not a day passes that I don't think about you.
Do you ever think of me, too?

I know I sound so needy.
I know I seem so insecure.
My best friend is what's missing.
Do you know how to get in touch with her?

Rainbow Bridge

Over the Rainbow Bridge way up in the sky,
there's a place that brings us comfort when we
have to say goodbye.

It's covered in paw prints galore
from the pets we loved and adored
that went beyond before you and I.
It has fields of green and streams of blue,
hills, trees, and flowers, too.
Beauty you can't deny.

Over the Rainbow Bridge way up in the sky,
there's a place where they never grow old, never
hurt, and never die.

They're young and spry.
They run and play.
They dig their holes and sleep all day.
Happiness all the time.
They chew their bones and scratch their nails.
They purr real loud and wag their tails.
It's just beyond our bridge of life.

Over the Rainbow Bridge way up in the sky,
they're safe and sound and patiently wait for us
just on the other side.

Grief

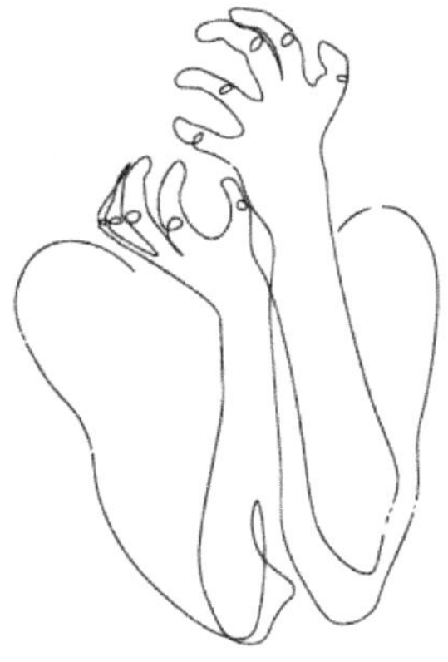

Fighting.
Struggling.
Barely staying afloat.
Sinking.
Drowning.
I've completely lost hope.

When will this feeling end?
Will it always be this way?
It suffocates me.
It lives rent-free throughout my body all night,
every day.

It depletes me.
It consumes me.
It's taken ahold.

It's now my identity.
The parasite vs. the host.

All my joy has vanished.
My laugh is solely a sham.
I wear a mask to hide the truth.
I'm no longer who I say I am.

Physically, I'm intact.
Emotionally, I'm shattered.
Mentally, I'm drained.
My thoughts are utterly scattered.

With outward appearances, I'm held together
nicely;
I'm no different from who I was before.
On the inside, it's quite the disarray.
I've been stripped down and deprived to my very
core.

I've met the hurt before, and I was acquainted
with the ache;
this isn't a first for me.
This time it's a different pain;
a more severe degree.
There was never an opportunity to save myself;
every option was void and denied.
I've succumbed to the virus completely.
I was infected the day you died.

After

After the soul leaves the body and life is no
more,
After all that's left is a lifeless vessel for all to
mourn,
The phone calls begin and the text messages
ensue,
The promises of prayers begin and the "I'm
always here for you."

After the services have been planned and the
choice of casket or urn is made,
After the headstone has been picked along with
the plot for the grave,
Prayers are still promised and calls still take
place,
There are stories from strangers, and hugs from
friends who wipe the tears from your face.

After the eulogy has been read and the
preacher's prayer has been prayed,

After the hearse is loaded along with the flowers
on sprays,
One by one, you're escorted through the doors,
The reality sets in that your life before is no
more.

After the procession is lined up and all are
cemetery-bound,
After your loved one is lowered into the cold,
hard ground,
Once again the "I love you's" begin and more
promises of prayers to be prayed...
But they get to leave, and you're left to face the
grief that doesn't fade.

After the days begin to pass and the weeks go
by,
After you feel like you're constantly reliving the
worst day of your life,
After you realize that you're completely numb
and feel everything all at once,
After the nightmare never ends and you can
never wake up,
After grief steals all your joy and is replaced by
sorrow,
After you have no choice but to face every
tomorrow,
After the calls stop and the text messages end,

After you just go through the motions and just
have to pretend,
After days go by that turn to weeks, months, and
eventually years,
After grief consumes you completely...
Who will still be here?

Griever's Advice

Take all the pictures you can take.
Make all the memories you can make.
Say all the "I love you's" you can say.
Make the time to get away.

Save all the voicemails you can save.
Play all the games that you can play.
I wish I had,
now it's too late.

Do it now.
Do it today.
Time is precious.
Please, don't wait.

Take my advice.
Heed my words.
Talk is cheap,
but the world is absurd.

Life can change in the blink of an eye.
Loved ones are gone,
and you never get to say goodbye.
All you'll have left are stills in frames,
you'll need them to get through the rest of your
days.

You can lose them,
no matter day or night.
Hold them close.
Hold them tight.

I didn't and I hesitated.
Never once had I anticipated.
Foolish for thinking I had plenty of time.
Fed myself so many lies.

Now he's gone and I'm still here.
Never thought he'd disappear.
It's not fair how he died; not fair how he left.
Taken too soon.
Death is theft.

Daddy

I've always been obsessed with the red, orange,
and yellow flames.
It's ironic how my obsession is what took my
father to his early grave.
I wasn't there when it happened.
There wasn't anything I could have done.
I still feel this weight of guilt because of the
unspoken words left on my tongue.

I hope he knew how much I loved him.
I really hope he knew.
He was never one to talk about feelings;
rare were the words "I love you".
I blame it on his raising,
like a prisoner, he was denied affection.
Favoritism was placed towards his siblings;
a sick game of selection.

I hope he knew how much I admired him.
I really hope he had a clue.
Always he'll be my Daddy.
Always my hero, too.
Never the only and never the last,
but the absolute greatest man I've ever known.
Never one to be found in the future, present, or
past.
Simply put, he broke the mold.

I hope he knew that nobody can fill his shoes but
him,
I really hope he seen.
An all-knowing, constant provider
with a sharp mind; very keen.
A modern knight in shining armor;
the hardworking, laid-back, boot-wearing,
flannel-clad farmer.

I hope he knew that he could never be replaced.
Never will he be while I'm still alive.
If I could have changed the way things played
out,
he never would have died.
Out he would have walked from the
smoke-filled, fire-consumed home,
but instead, he made the incorrect decision and
had to die alone.

If a sacrifice was needed, I would have let his
life go on.
Because I loved him so much, for him, I would
have given up my own.

Thoughts of the Infertile

I can tell my time is coming to a close -
the time to have a child of my own.
You say I should just adopt,
but there's no "just" to it.
Please, I really wish you'd stop.

I fight with my demons every day.
I try to ignore what they have to say.
I tell myself "I am enough" like I've been told to
do,
but I've never been able to believe that it's true.

I feel all alone in a crowded room.
You can't relate to me.
I can't relate to you.

My body doesn't do the one thing it's made to
do.
I never thought I'd feel so broken and empty.
I just wonder why God doesn't like me.

I knew a big family was what I always wanted.
It's sad that infertility has caused that growth to
be stunted.
Now, it's him and me, and me and him, and an
unhealthy number of pets.
I'll never understand why he's not left me yet.

I feel all alone in a crowded room.
You can't relate to me.
I can't relate to you.
My body doesn't do the one thing it's made to
do.
I never thought I'd still feel so broken and
empty.
I just wonder what I've done to make God not
like me.

At once there was a light at the end of the
tunnel,
but as the years have gone by it's now like
looking through a funnel.
I keep asking God when it will be our turn.
I guess some things we're just not meant to
learn.

The thought of us growing old alone makes me
feel guilty and sad.
Some days I'm okay with it,
other days I'm just mad.
Phrases of "when we" and "if we" are being used
less and less.
I hate that he's stuck with me and I'm such a
broken mess.

I'm all alone in a crowded room.
You can't relate to me.
I can't relate to you.
My body doesn't do the one thing it's made to
do.
I never thought I'd always feel so broken and
empty.
I just wonder what I've done to make God not
like me.

Burning House

Our family home,
GONE.
Destroyed by flames.
Everything taken,
by an unforgiving blaze.

Memory-covered walls,
standing tall, strong, and unadjust,
have now crumbled down,
leaving only charred dust.

The shingle-clad roof,
made to protect and shield,
has now caved in,
completely unsealed.

Windows clear,
made of glass,
once allowing light and air to enter,
now broken, busted, shattered, and cracked,

nonaligned,
off-centered.

The floors of carpet and wood,
top of the line,
created with stability and design,
now burnt, seared, torched, and destroyed.
Dilapidated.
Entirely void.

Missing are the beds that held our weary souls,
tables that hosted card games aplenty,
corded phones that heard gossip-filled
conversations,
along with the cedar chest that kept safe our
precious heirlooms and memories.

Departed are the closets that stored holiday
decor,
cabinets that protected our valued collections,
cases that held books of knowledge,
the pantry filled with baking confections.

The fiery blaze was hungry,
shown by clearing the foundation,
but it was greedy and took more than our
material possessions.
The torturing hell took my loving father,
a moment in time I wish I could alter.

The savage inferno took it all.
It showed no mercy in its path.
It devoured all happiness, hopes, security, and
dreams,
leaving behind a catastrophic aftermath.

Burning House, a symbol of sorrow,
a reminder to cherish all time spent.
In the blink of an eye, everything we know can
suddenly change,
but the memories we hold will forever remain.

Through a Child's Mind

I never had a tree with branches spread far apart;
there wasn't a clubhouse built up inside.
I used the whole farm as my playground.
There were so many places to run and hide!

I fought monsters and dragons,
somehow I won every time.
A tobacco stick was my sword.
My shield was whatever I could find.

I came over on the Mayflower.
It was a heck of a trip!
It was rough navigating the seas,
when using a feeding trough for a ship!

I was on the run, disguised as a guy.
Running from my mean husband; I couldn't
afford a divorce!
I changed my name, changed my age.
I got around on my two-wheeled horse!

I'd sneak into the feed room after feed had been
unbagged,
I'd do it as soon as Daddy turned his back.
I'd roll in the dusty pellet crushed corn.
I'd make snow angels on the feed room floor.

Weekly concerts were held in the barn.
The old wagon was my private stage.
Pigs and cattle were my unpaying patrons.
My backdrop was made of square bales of hay.

I knew to stay out of the hayloft as the floor
wasn't completely stable.
Many times, this I was told.
Never was I the one to listen.
This superhero couldn't be controlled!

I'd sneak away and go up on the hill -
the place I was not supposed to be alone.
All I had to do was not get caught,
I should have known my cover would be
eventually blown!

Fossils, fairies, Bigfoot, and gnomes,
if anyone could find them, it'd be me!
I did find some pretty cool rocks!
I officially called off the search for the other
three.

I remember the laughter and the silly games I'd
play,
running barefoot through the grass on a hot
summer day,
catching lightning bugs and climbing rocks,
paying no mind to the passing time on the clock.

I was the only child until age ten,
I had many make-believe friends.
We'd build a fort in my world of pretend.
My lone imagination knew no end.

Time quickly passes and puerility fades,
some memories linger and some become hazed.
Though years march on and I grow old,
I'll always keep close the stories untold.

Precious are the days not so long ago,
when the world was filled with only fun and
magic.
I now see the world through anguish and
heartbreak,
all fueled by death so tragic.

Puff Puff Pass

He who rolls it, lights it.
Pass it around.
No triple hits,
don't hog that shit,
don't let the fire go out.
Puff, puff, pass.

This ain't the weed you used to know.
We've got weed for all your needs.
It'll make you eat,
it'll make you sleep,
this shit will make you think.
Puff, puff, pass.

We've got weed from Cali,
weed from 'Rado,
and weed from Detroit City.
This weed doesn't have any seeds or stems.
This green is downright pretty.
Puff, puff, pass.

It'll get you high,
it'll make you fly,
it'll give you the munchies,
it'll knock you down to the ground.
Man, this couch lock has grabbed me.
Puff, puff, pass.

Break it.
Grind it.
Roll it.
Smoke.
One hit.
Two hits.
You don't get off until you choke.

Break it.
Grind it.
Pack a bowl.
One hit.
Two hits.
Don't stop until you're stoned.

I don't need your damn coffee.
I don't want your wine.
Every day I got that wake-and-bake,
it's got me feeling fine.
Puff, puff, pass.

He who rolls it, lights it.
Pass it around...

Happy New Year No More

December has the bearded man in the bright red
suit,
November has family and friends gathered
around a table of food.
October has costume parties with endless treats
and tricks,
September has over-the-top tailgating and
football game picks.
August is summer's sad official end,
July has firework shows and cookouts to attend.
June is the month for elaborate wedding
celebrations,
May is the month of many graduations.
April is known for all the rain showers,
March is the month that time springs forward an
hour.
February is for celebrating love so true,

January is filled with promises of all things
anew.
For me, January will always be the month I lost
you.

The Old Barn

On our old family farm where weeds now grow,
stands an old weathered barn with stories untold.
The timbers are worn and the roof is covered in
moss,
for nearly a century it has stood through both
gain and loss.

The walls are a patchwork quilt made of wood.
Each plank tells a story - either bad or good.
Where tobacco once cured and cattle did graze,
now stands an empty relic of many past days.

This old farm was once active with new life,
but now it's just a memory filled with strife.
The farmer who took care of it has now passed;
disappeared.
But the barn still stands proud year after year.

When the doors open, they creak on rusty
hinges,
as if to welcome back the ghosts of past images.
The hayloft is empty; the stalls lie bare,
as memories linger in the cool, musty air.

The wind whistles through the cracks in the
walls,
as the old barn watches the raindrops fall.
Today, on the farm it still stands, a silent
sentinel,
a testament to the days when it was essential.

Dear old barn, standing solid and strong,
you've weathered many storms, for either right
or wrong.
Though you may be forgotten, you will never be
gone.
The old barn will continue to stand, unfaltering
and lifelong.

Have You

Have you found your Daddy?
The man I never got to meet.
Did he usher you through the pearly gates?
Did he save you a seat?
Together you'll be farming the fields of Heaven
forevermore,
raising cattle, tobacco, hay, and corn.
Have you found your Daddy?
I know he was the man you always mourned.

Have you found Haggard?
I know you loved to hear him sing.
You always smiled a mile wide listening to
"Mama Tried" and "Silver Wings".

Your favorite was "If We Make it Through
December".
Do you remember snapping your fingers and
tapping your feet?
Have you found Haggard?
I hope you've had the chance to meet.

Have you found Jim Varney?
You loved his movies of humor and wit.
From 'Scared Stupid' to 'Saves Christmas',
you could be found engaged in his comical skit.
Have you shared stories about your contentment
and strife?
Have you talked about your girls?
Have you told him about your wife?
Have you found Jim Varney?
I hope you're living your best afterlife.

Have you found the Rainbow Bridge?
You've always missed your four-legged
companions that went on before.
Did they wait for you on the other side?
Did their excitement cause an uproar?
Were you greeted by wagging tails and nuzzled
by wet noses?
Have they followed you every paw step in
stride?
Have you found the Rainbow Bridge?

I know they'd always be faithful both earthbound
and on Heaven's side.

Have you met God?
An absurd question, I'm sure.
Is He mellow and outgoing?
Is He strict and stern?
Have you asked Him why in that manner?
Have you asked Him why you had to go away?
Have you met God?
Oh, how I wish He would have allowed you to
stay.

Revision

I never imagined it would happen this way -
the way you died.
I'd always hoped you'd go in your sleep,
but fate was unkind.

You never imagine it'll happen to your family,
such a loss of a tragic degree.
You hear of it affecting strangers,
thinking "it could never happen to me."

You relive the nightmare -
every time you close your eyes.
Though, events of the day are missing,
lost in the soul-crushing news of your demise.

"Everything happens for a reason."
Those words I've always believed.

As hard as I've tried, I've been unable to find any
fair or right reason why you had to leave.

It's not just that you died that bothers me,
it's the manner in which you were taken.
It keeps me up at night.
My world's left totally shattered and shaken.

Death is the one thing certain in this life,
regardless of the means.
Sometimes bitter and cruel, fate is not always
sweet.
If possible, I would have intervened,
I would have changed the timeline's course.
Your life wouldn't have ended.
I wouldn't be out of sorts.

For the rest of my life I'll always feel
remorseful.
The feeling that I could have somehow changed
this will eternally haunt me.
Peace and contentment I'll experience
nevermore.
My life entirely altered in January of twenty
twenty-four.

Realization

I long to live as a modern-day hippie,
walking barefoot and carefree,
draped in tie-dye, compassion, and mercy,
surviving off the land and smoking the green.

Instead, I'm forced to sell my soul to the
money-green devil.
He owns me for as long as I'm able.
It would be ideal to end the contract,
but I have to put food on the table.

We could be living our best lives:
shroom hunting, beach bumming;
really living life to the max!
Instead, we're constrained to barely livable
wages, credit scores, and income tax.

How long is this rat race going to run?
Why does it take place inside an enclosed cage?
Little by little, more of our freedoms are stolen,
then they're surprised when they're met with
rage.

The forty-hour workweek is a scam.
It's solely fueled by corporate greed and lies.
Honesty is lost on the higher end of the ladder.
Maybe death IS the final prize.

Fishing with Daddy

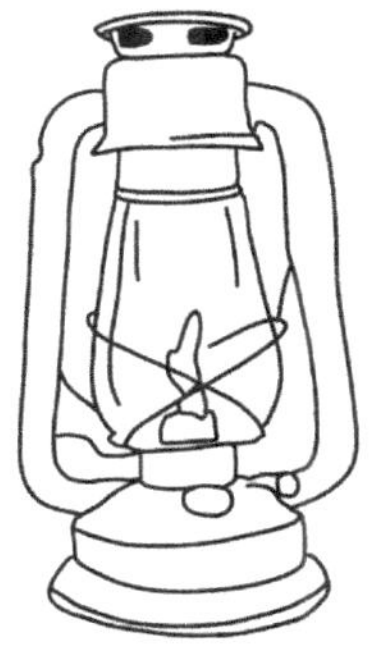

He bought my first rod for me on a whim.
I was so excited to be just like him!
It was brightly colored yellow and white.
At barely three feet long, it fit in my small hands
just right.

Into the rich earth, we'd dig for bait.
Going fishing with my Daddy, I could hardly
wait!
He taught me how to correctly hook the worm.
Being a tomboy at heart, I wasn't bothered when
it squirmed.

With patience, he showed me how to cast and
reel.
When I finally succeeded, it was a big ordeal!

We used buckets for seats as we sat next to the
lake.
On the hotter days in the sun, we'd really bake!

He told me that we had to stay quiet because fish
knew when we're being loud,
all that wisdom and I still managed to run my
mouth.
I asked him if he ever fished with his Dad.
He told me about the biggest catch they ever
had.

We watched the water ripple as we cast the line,
we'd sit there for hours basking in the sunshine.
We'd watch the bobbers dance on the water's
crown,
I wished we could forever stay by the
fisherman's playground.

The time would pass, turning day to night,
he'd then pull out his lantern to use for light.
When we were finally content with our
gilled-catch,
we'd gather our gear and then release our batch.

Fishing with Daddy wasn't for food or
competition,
it was a short-lived weekend tradition.

Here's to the memories we made out by the
water,
fishing together - my father and his daughter.
From every cast and every line,
I'll cherish these memories for all time.

One Day

I'm mad that we're here alone.
Together on this unfamiliar path, we're left to
roam.
He was our fearless leader;
our sense of direction.
He was our home and heart;
our source of protection.

He was our electrician and plumber,
our provider and farmer.
She was his wife.
We were his daughters.

I believe we deserved a chance to say goodbye;
to share our farewells face-to-face.

Mostly, his ashes are underground,
the rest are stored in a vase.

It happened so quickly.
He was gone in an instant.
Nothing about it is right or fair;
here and then gone the next minute.

There was no chance to see his body at peace;
laying in eternal sleep.
No suit and tie to pick out; no casket for his rest.
Our options were limited, but for him, only the
very best.

One day when we meet again, I'll know exactly
where to find him...
On an old Ford tractor plowing Heaven's golden
fields is where he'll be.
When I find him, there'll be no more goodbyes.
He'll finally be next to me.

Cry

I cry all the time.
Once I'm awake,
then myself back to sleep.
I don't know how to be me anymore.
Happy moments make me weep.

I cry out for you.
It doesn't make a difference;
I know you're not here.
I've cried so much I don't know how I still have
any tears.

I cry for our past.
Our family's future was torn apart;
ripped to shreds.
Milestones and holidays that I used to look
forward to are now something I completely
dread.

I cry because I can't see you.
It haunts me because it's been so long since the
last time I saw your face.
I look for your face amongst strangers;
in every empty seat, every blank space.

I cry because I can't hear you.
The things I'd give to hear your laugh just once
more...
The things I'd do to have things back to the way
they were before...

I cry because I'm afraid I'll forget.
Forget your face, your voice, your favorite
things, and your favorite foods.
I just wish I could cry you back to life, then I
wouldn't be able to forget you.

Lessons

The hardest phone call I've ever had to make,
was to tell my baby sister that our Daddy went
away.

The hardest part about looking into my
Momma's broken eyes,
was knowing that she had to watch helplessly as
her life crumbled down around her while my
Daddy met his untimely demise.

The hardest choice I've ever had to help choose,
was what urn we wanted to use.

The hardest words I've ever had to receive,
were your obituary read aloud - it was
something I wanted so badly to not believe.

The hardest thing I've ever had to see,
was your urn being lowered into the ground.
That's a pain of a different degree.

The hardest thing I've ever had to accept,
is that you're no longer here.
Understanding it is a terribly hard concept.

The hardest thing I'll ever have to do,
is learn to live the rest of my life without you.

Family Feud

Death can either bring a family together or tear
one apart.
With my father's death, it definitely hasn't helped
rectify our situation.
Emotions run high and words are
misunderstood;
before you know it, it's a full-blown
confrontation!

Our small family has never been picture-perfect.
Oh no! Far from it, to say the least.
Never the smiling faces on Christmas card
photos,
we're more like a dysfunctional jigsaw puzzle -
now missing a piece.

We argue, fuss, yell, and scream.
We point fingers, cry, and blame.
Fine one moment, mad the next.
You never know - it's always a guessing game.

Our relationship isn't healthy.
But we love one another just the same.
It's a wonder that we're still allowed to roam the
streets freely.
If people really knew, we'd be diagnosed
borderline insane.

I laugh and joke about our situation
because this is the way it's always went.
It's hard to imagine a "normal" family
because this is how our time has always been
spent.

This is not the way to be.
Daddy wouldn't want us to act this way.
Truthfully, I'm tired of playing mediator,
but I can't just give up and walk away.

We all have issues that are unaddressed.
We all need to reflect on the way we act.
None of us are perfect - not even in the way we
think and speak.
We only hear what we want and then have the
audacity to overreact.

I wonder how Daddy put up with the three of us
for so long.
I wonder how he still had any sense.
I'm already at wits' end.
I'm over the situation always being tense.

My medication isn't strong enough for this.
Is it too much to ask for everyone to try to
compromise?
I don't know if I can deal with this for much
longer.
There's no reason to always instigate or
antagonize.

We're supposed to be a family.
If Daddy knew about all of this, he'd be in total
disbelief.
After death, one experiences many stages.
I never knew being hard-headed and stubborn
were stages of grief.

Ladder of Depressed

Wake up.
Go to work.
Climbing that ladder,
barely putting food on the table,
helping the rich man's wallet get fatter.

Slowly killing ourselves,
all for that mighty dollar.
Letting the clock on the wall,
count away the minutes of our life.
Allowing a job to control the balance of earning
a living and spending time with your kids and
wife.

"You're doing a great job!"
In the end, that just earns you more work to
complete.

You're steady and reliable.
Wake. Work. Home. Repeat.

More work to complete,
the same deadline as before.
No increase in pay.
Nope, that's not something they can afford!

Your hours are extended;
your days off are cut short.
"Don't let us down!"
"We always count on you for support!"

They never comment on the work you do.
No, they take that for granted.
They sure have something to say if you make a
mistake.
They promote others overlooking your efforts.
"If we promote you, there'd be no one to take
your place!

You start to quit -
doing so quietly to see if they take note.
They don't see that you're miserable;
barely staying afloat.

Clock in; clock out.
Day after day.
Slowly dying inside;

wasting away.

A job that you once loved is now something you
hate.
You dread going in every single day.
You're sick to your stomach and your head hurts
all the time.
You have to support your family;
can't let the bills get behind.

You're steady and reliable.
All your resources gradually deplete.
Doing it until you die.
Wake. Work. Home. Repeat.

Weed

Everybody has their own way to grieve.
We all have our own way to cope.
Some people turn to food, pills, or alcohol.
Some like to roll up smoke.

It's branded as something terrible.
You're looked down on if you partake;
you're seen as a lazy bum without ambition.
It's been around since the beginning of time.
By now, marijuana should be a celebrated
tradition!

It's okay to relax with a glass of wine.
It's socially acceptable to unwind with a beer.
It's a problem to smoke something natural;
I'm not sure why it's something so many people
fear.

It should be legalized countrywide so we can all
enjoy the beautiful green.

The government knows that they won't be able
to capitalize on the means.
They're in the drug companies' pockets and
make money from filled jail cells.
They're adding fuel to fire using lies because
they know fear sells.

In the meantime, roll that joint,
or pack your bowl.
Legal or not, there are some things the
government won't be able to control.

Do what you need to do to help you survive your
grief and cope.
Even if it's packing another bowl and taking
another toke.
Do what you have to do.
Priority first: Take care of you.
After all, weed is self-care, too.

Why

Why didn't you come out of the house?
These words haunt every fiber of my being.
You opened the door for Momma.
Why didn't you take her lead?

Why didn't you come out of the house?
I ask this question every single day.
There was nothing there worth saving.
To have you back, all of it I would easily trade.

Why didn't you come out of the house?
They said they found your body six to eight feet
from the back door.
Had you already turned back around to come
outside?
Or is that as far as you made it before you
collapsed to the floor?

Why didn't you come out of the house?
This I cry every time I hold your ashes in my
hands.
I know we'll never know the reason.
I know I will never understand.

Why didn't you come out of the house?
This shouldn't have been the way you took your
last breath.
Were you just destined to die so horribly?
Your father also died a tragic death.

Why didn't you come out of the house?
This question will haunt me until the day I die.
I scream it to the heavens.
I will always wonder why.

The Last Time

He always wanted a son until Momma babysat
those mean little boys down the road.
I guess I worried him half to death because
everywhere he went I was "Daddy, I wanna go."

I was his little shadow, following him every step
for step.
From the barnyard to the stock barn and
everywhere in between,
I was always on his heels,
there was no getting rid of me.

Then one day it was the last time,
the last time we went to the barn.
One day it was the last time,
the last time out on the farm.

You never think it'll end.
We're gonna do it again.
Don't know when,
we'll have to wait and see...
But the last time was the last time...
for me.

He bought me my first rod and reel,
and then later my first set of wheels.
Those wheels never fell off but that motor
finally blew.
Just like him, they don't make them the way they
used to.

He was never one to let us help,
if something needed to be done,
he'd do it himself.
I was only allowed to hand over the screwdriver
or hold the flashlight.
Like him, I'm always late and stay up all night.

Time quickly passes and seasons change,
and you fail to realize as you age,
so do they.
Time spent together is like gold,
you try every way to keep holding on.
Still things happen out of your control.

Then one day it was the last time,
the last time I saw his face.
One day it was the last time,
the last time I heard his words "Stay safe."
You never think it'll end.
You're going to see him again.
Don't know when,
we'll have to wait and see...
But the last time was the last time...
for me.

Trip to Heaven

It's very cliche to wish that Heaven had visiting
hours,
but I'd wait as long as needed without complaint.
Long-distance travel charges?
I'd pay any amount demanded.
Money wouldn't be a restraint.

You'd introduce me to your Daddy, and together
we'd walk down the streets of gold.
Together, you would tell me forgotten stories
from the days of old.

Later, we'd walk down to the fields, and I'd
admire the freshly broken earth you just plowed,
then we would head over to the barn to see your
heavenly herd of dairy cows.

Upon an old wagon, we'd sit and talk for hours.
You'd tell me how you've been;
that your body's like new.
I wouldn't speak.
I'd just take it all in.

I'd eagerly listen to your stories that you've told
me time after time.
I'd memorize your voice and the lines on your
face.
I'd inhale your cologne and squeeze you tight in
our farewell embrace.

I'd assure you that I will be back again; time or
travel wouldn't be an issue.
"I'll take the day off work and bring the family
because they sure do miss you."

Visiting hours are a nice thought, even if it's just
to pacify the time,
I know the real places to visit are the corners of
my mind.
Inside are all the memories of you that I'll keep
safely locked and sealed up tight,

but the day I get to see you again will truly be a beautiful sight!

Growing Through Grief

In the aftermath of a loss, we find ourselves in disbelief,
as we attempt to navigate the unknown turbulent waters of our newfound grief.
It's a heavy burden that constantly weighs down our soul.
It's a daily struggle to find ways that our broken heart can be consoled.

It's a tangled mess of emotions as grief is not a linear path,
it twists and turns with vengeance and rage with its depth of wrath.

Although the road is rough and rocky, we
blindly press on,
we try to adjust to this new life that we wake up
to with every new dawn.

The pain runs deep; a constant ache,
it's a sorrowful song we cannot shake.
We have no choice but to discover our way
through the grief.
It's our personal journey through darkness
searching for relief.

With tears and anguish, we learn to cope,
we grow stronger with every shimmer of hope.
It's a process of healing, slow but assured,
finding solace in the memories and moments
that we've endured.

Grief is a journey of healing, acceptance, and
growth,
down through the valleys of sadness and over
the peaks of hope.
We not only emerge stronger, but we also
emerge whole,
in the depths of grief, we find our true role.

So embrace the pain and the tears,
because through them we conquer our deepest,
darkest fears.

In the midst of sorrow, we find our strength,
becoming stronger and more resilient, we go to
great lengths.

Continue to honor the ones we've lost along the
way,
allow their spirit to live on in our hearts every
day.
Learn to cherish every moment and every single
breath,
proceed to love in life and in death.
Hold on to love and remember with grace,
Growing Through Grief, we find our place.